Making the Most of Standards

The Sustainability Professional's Guide

Adrian Henriques

Visiting Professor of Accountability and CSR

Middlesex University Business School

First published in 2012 by Dō Sustainability
87 Lonsdale Road, Oxford OX2 7ET, UK

ISBN 978-1-909293-25-0 (eBook-ePub)
ISBN 978-1-909293-26-7 (eBook-PDF)
ISBN 978-1-909293-24-3 (Paperback)

A catalogue record for this title is available from the British Library.

At Dō Sustainability we strive to minimize our environmental impacts and carbon footprint through reducing waste, recycling and offsetting our CO_2 emissions, including those created through publication of this book. For more information on our environmental policy see **www.dosustainability.com**.

Page design and typesetting by Alison Rayner
Cover by Becky Chilcott

For further information on Dō Sustainability, visit our website:
www.dosustainability.com

DōShorts

Dō Sustainability is the publisher of **DōShorts**: short, high-value ebooks that distil sustainability best practice and business insights for busy, results-driven professionals. Each DōShort can be read in 90 minutes.

New and forthcoming DōShorts -- stay up to date

We publish 3 to 5 new DōShorts each month. The best way to keep up to date? Sign up to our short, monthly newsletter. Go to **www. dosustainability.com/newsletter** to sign up to the Dō Newsletter. Some of our latest and forthcoming titles include:

- *Green Jujitsu: Embed Sustainability into Your Organisation* Gareth Kane
- *How to Make your Company a Recognised Sustainability Champion* Brendan May
- *Making the Most of Standards* Adrian Henriques
- *Promoting Sustainable Behaviour: A Practical Guide to What Works* Adam Corner
- *Solar Photovoltaics Business Briefing* David Thorpe
- *Sustainability in the Public Sector* Sonja Powell
- *Sustainability Reporting for SMEs* Elaine Cohen
- *Sustainable Transport Fuels Business Briefing* David Thorpe
- *The Changing Profile of Corporate Climate Change Risk* Mark Trexler & Laura Kosloff
- *The First 100 Days: Plan, Prioritise & Build a Sustainable Organisation* Anne Augustine
- *The Short Guide to SRI* Cary Krosinsky

Subscriptions

In additional to individual sales and rentals, we offer organisational subscriptions to our full collection of published and forthcoming books. To discuss a subscription for your organisation, email **veruschka@dosustainability.com**

Write for us, or suggest a DōShort

Please visit **www.dosustainability.com** for our full publishing programme. If you don't find what you need, write for us! Or Suggest a DōShort on our website. We look forward to hearing from you.

Abstract

THE WORLD OF CORPORATE RESPONSIBILITY STANDARDS is large and confusing. There are so many standards of different kinds that it is bewildering for someone trying to find an appropriate sustainability standard for their company or organisation.

This short book cuts through the confusion. It explains:

1. The variety of standards out there

2. The pros and cons of using standards to improve sustainability performance

3. A map showing how some of the most prominent sustainability standards relate to each other

4. For some of the most influential standards, a thumbnail description of what they are actually about

5. A decision tree to help with choosing the type of standard that may be most helpful to you

6. Some tips for putting standards into practice.

About the Author

 **ADRIAN HENRIQUES** is an adviser on corporate responsibility, social accountability and sustainability. He was for five years a member of the Global Reporting Initiative Steering Committee and has been a Council Member of AccountAbility. Adrian is also a member of the Association of Chartered Certified Accountants' Sustainability Forum and Chair of the UK mirror committee for ISO 26000. He has been involved in the development of many standards. He is Visiting Professor of Accountability and CSR at Middlesex University Business School. He was formerly Head of Accountability at the New Economics Foundation and has also worked for the International Society for Ecology and Culture, an NGO campaigning on economic globalisation. For a number of years prior to that Adrian was a management consultant for PriceWaterhouseCoopers in financial services.

His publications include:

- 2012. *Standards for Change: ISO 26000 and Sustainable Development* (London: IIED)

- 2011. *Understanding ISO 26000: A Practical Approach to Social Responsibility* (London: BSI)

- 2010. *Corporate Impact: Measuring and Managing Your Social Footprint* (London: Earthscan)

- 2009. Ethical codes at work. In: Spitzeck, H., Pirson, M., Amann, W., Khan, S. and v. Kimakowitz, E. (eds) *Humanism in Business* (Cambridge: Cambridge University Press)

web: **www.henriques.info**

Contents

Abstract...5

About the Author 7

Introduction...13

1 The Variety of Standards 15

    Who says so?..15

    What do they say?... 17

    What are they about?.......................................18

    How do you know? 18

        Is certifiability a good idea?...........................19

    Having parties 21

    Labels and initiatives.....................................21

    Types of standard 22

2 Pros and Cons of Standards 23

3 A Map of Standards 25

4 Standards...27

    Fundamental standards 28

        Human rights...28

        Labour rights 30

Broad spectrum standards...................................33

   Global Compact: Sustainability aspiration..................33

   OECD Guidelines for Multinational Enterprises...........37

Organisational practice standards 41

   AA1000: Report assurance 42

   GRI: Reporting 46

   ISO 14001: Environmental management...................50

   ISO 26000: Social responsibility 53

Special purpose standards.......................................58

   Fairtrade: Producers 58

   FSC: Wood 62

   PRI: Investment 66

   SA8000: Supply chain..................................69

   Voluntary Principles: Security........................72

5   Decision time..75

6   Putting Standards into Practice.......................77

Get involved before the standard even exists! 77

Use the standard implementation process
as an awareness-raising exercise 78

Is the standard good enough?...........................78

But it can be a slog...................................79

How do you know the standard is making
a difference?..79

Ask your friends – and enemies.........................80

Integrate the standard into the business strategy.....81

Do standards, but think stakeholders............................81

How do standards affect each other?........................82

Make a difference!...83

Introduction

STANDARDS ARE SUPPOSED TO HELP YOU do something better without re-inventing the wheel. But the world of sustainability standards is large and confusing. There are a great many standards covering various kinds of social and environmental impacts, with somewhat fewer addressing economic impacts. There are also standards that try to cover all aspects of sustainability. And standards tend to generate other standards: if there is a standard for environmental issues and one for social issues, the temptation is to produce another standard that covers both. But instead of replacing the first two standards, the new one simply becomes a third and adds to the confusion. This is one of the ways that the number of sustainability standards has mushroomed in recent years and served to put people off standards altogether.

All of this is odd because the very word 'standard' suggests that there should be only one for any given topic. Standardisation for some topics (perhaps the dimensions of a screw thread) does tend to produce a single standard. Standards for sustainability are not like that. The section on the 'Variety of standards' describes what they are like. In this way, books on standards, like standards themselves, can make things worse as well as better. This book is simply trying to provide a map or some basic orientation to the world of standards. As a result it cannot claim to be definitive: there are many hundreds of sustainability standards out there. Of course, they are of varying quality and some are little used.

So this book describes:

1. The variety of standards out there

2. The pros and cons of using standards to improve sustainability performance

3. A map showing how some of the most prominent sustainability standards relate to each other

4. For some of the most influential standards, a thumbnail description of what they are actually about

5. A decision tree to help with choosing the type of standard that may be most helpful to you

6. Some tips for putting standards into practice.

....

CHAPTER 1

The Variety of Standards

A STANDARD IS AN AGREED SET OF CHARACTERISTICS, including ways of behaving or doing something. Often the agreed way of doing something arises out of common practice – standards for technical areas like the specification of screw threads are an example. But when talking about sustainability, often standards are a way of trying to achieve common practice in an area in which it may not yet widely exist, such as the measurement of carbon dioxide emissions.

The topic of standards is complex as there are many varieties and ways of classifying and understanding them. This section takes a functional approach, asking questions such as 'what do they do?' and 'how do they do it?'

Who says so?

Perhaps the most important aspect of a standard is 'who says' that it is a good way to do things. This governs the legitimacy of the standard.

By numbers, the majority of standards have been produced by ISO (the International Standards Organisation) or its members, the national standards bodies. There are tens of thousands of ISO standards alone, mostly covering technical activities that have been agreed principally by commercial organisations. However, there are some important ISO standards very relevant to sustainability, including ISO 14001 on environmental management systems and ISO 26000 on organisational social responsibility.

Other standards have been produced by civil society. These include many of the prominent standards for particular aspects of sustainability. Fairtrade (principally for ensuring socially acceptable standards of production) is an example.

The public sector can also produce standards. Some of these concern the operational activities of the public sector itself, while others are the result of the political process. Those standards resulting from the political process are called 'laws' or regulations. (Standards produced by non-state actors are therefore often described as 'voluntary regulation' or 'self-regulation'.) At the international level, the laws become treaties. For sustainability, some of the most important standards include the human rights and the ILO (International Labour Organisation) conventions labour rights.

Standards can sometimes 'move' from one sponsor to another. Standards for organic food were originally produced by civil society but are now supported by governments. Other standards produced by civil society will incorporate elements such as labour rights within them: SA8000 on labour conditions is an example.

Given that the answer to the question 'who says so' governs the legitimacy of the standard, it follows that the most powerful standards, from the point of view of legitimacy, are those which have included all sectors and many different parties in their development and maintenance. The FSC standard (for sustainable wood products) is a good example.

What do they say?

There are two big groups of standards: guidance standards and specification standards. Most people naturally assume that all standards dictate certain practices. Standards that don't dictate something may not really feel like standards. However, many standards relevant to sustainability are guidance standards of just this kind. That means they provide recommendations, but do not specify requirements that have to be met. And there is no mechanism for proving that you have abided by the standard.

Guidance standards include types of standard like industry (or civil society or government) Codes of Practice. Others express aspirations for ideal behaviour. The Global Compact, which sets out a series of economic, social and environmental aspirations, is an example of this type.

Specification standards set requirements for how things must be. These have to be written very precisely so that it is possible to tell whether or not things have actually been done as prescribed. This makes them especially boring, technical documents – whatever their worth in relation to sustainability. ISO 14001 and OHSAS 18001 (for health and safety systems) are specification standards. Many specification standards also contain elements of guidance.

Another useful distinction between different standards is between those that concern the process of managing something and those that describe the actual sustainability performance of a company. An example of a process standard would be ISO 14001, which is concerned with how environmental performance should be managed, but does not cover what performance should be aimed at. An example of a standard that describes actual performance would be ISO 26000 (at least in some areas). ISO 26000 covers many substantive issues including human rights, consumer marketing and community development.

What are they about?

The 'subject matter' of a standard is the set of characteristics that the standard is trying to standardise. For sustainability standards these may be social issues (such as the labour conditions of those cutting flowers), environmental issues (like the quantity of pollution an industrial process emits) or economic issues (including the extent of corruption). There are many standards that deal with very specific issues and products only, such as the Roundtable for Sustainable Palm Oil (RSPO).

How do you know?

The process for discovering whether or not an activity or product conforms to a specification ('requirements') standard, or complies with the law, is called variously 'monitoring', 'auditing' or 'providing assurance'.

The auditing process may result in a statement or certificate that gives the auditor's opinion on whether or not the standard has been followed. Such standards are called 'certifiable'. See the box below on whether this is a good idea.

The whole idea of applying standards may appear somewhat recursive. So, there are standards for auditing, such as AA1000 AS for auditing sustainability reports. Moreover, the process for determining who is qualified to be an auditor is sometimes itself standardised, when it is generally called 'accreditation'.

Is certifiability a good idea?

The proponents of certifiability argue that:

- The additional rigour with which requirements are specified (compared to recommendations for guidance) leads to greater attention to the issue and greater confidence in assessing progress, perhaps together with an increased chance of implementation activities to address the issue.

- Without the proof that certification provides, it is not possible for external parties to be sure that substantive performance is being improved and thereby hold organisations to account. Certification is therefore an indispensable tool with which to manage performance.

- Certification can offer a financial incentive for organisations that can demonstrate compliance by potentially differentiating themselves from their competitors.

The arguments against certifiability are that:

- The rigour necessary for specification can be misplaced, particularly for some of the social aspects of sustainable development. While the issues may be very real (e.g. sexual harassment) it can be very difficult to define appropriate and useful measures of the impact of actions intended to promote improvement. If requirements are nevertheless defined, it is likely that they may provide a misleading picture of the actual impact.

- It can lead to a culture of 'box-ticking', i.e. going through the motions of managing something without any real attention being paid to it.

- Certification creates significant additional costs.

SOURCE: From Henriques, A. 2012. Standards for Change: ISO 26000 and Sustainable Development (London: IIED, **http://pubs.iied.org/16513IIED.html**).

"HI! , I'M HERE TO CHECK YOUR AUDITING. SHE'S HERE TO CHECK MINE, THEN YOU HAVE TO CHECK HERS !"

© Maya Forstater

Having parties

Sometimes an organisation may check on its own performance in relation to a standard, as is required by ISO management systems. This is sometimes called 'first party' auditing. Large organisations may well have an internal department concerned with providing such 'internal audits'. When another organisation does it, it becomes a second party audit. This can happen when a purchasing organisation checks up on the sustainability performance of one of its suppliers. When someone who is independent of both organisations, in the sense that they have no direct interest in the outcome, does the auditing, it may be called 'third party' auditing.

However, the independence of an auditor will never be complete. Someone will be paying, and that is usually either the organisation itself or one of their suppliers.

Labels and initiatives

Labels are miniature, logo-like certificates typically attached to products, websites or reports. The organic label on a carton of milk is an example. The legal and commercial conditions for the use of a label are usually tightly controlled. Often a key condition of the use of a label is that the product has been sourced, manufactured or produced in accordance with a standard. This book is not concerned with labelling schemes directly, although two standards that underpin labels (Fairtrade and FSC) are described later.

Sustainability initiatives are projects with a sustainability purpose in mind. Sometimes that purpose will include the development of a standard that contributes to the ends that the initiative would like to achieve. Sometimes the standard is the sole product that the initiative is aiming at. Most of the standards described in this book are the result of the activities of an initiative.

Types of standard

There are many different sorts of sustainability standard that may be relevant to an organisation. This section describes some of the more prominent standards in brief. There is no single, completely satisfactory way to classify standards. For example, a standard may be broad in one sense (covering all aspects of sustainability) but designed only for a particular sector; or designed for all sectors but focusing only on one aspect for sustainability.

CHAPTER 2

Pros and Cons of Standards

SUSTAINABILITY STANDARDS HAVE DETRACTORS as well as champions. There are cogent arguments on both sides. The advantages and disadvantages are summarised below.

The advantages of standards are:

- *Good advice.* They provide a source of good practice. In whatever the area of standardisation, the advice or requirements within the standard can help with sound ways of dealing with sustainability issues. Depending on the particular standard, this could include environmental issues, human rights or labour practices, for example.

- *Gain business.* They can be a condition of doing business. If your customer demands adherence to a standard (or else they won't buy from you) then following a standard becomes a condition of business. This sort of pressure tends to follow the supply chain. The international standard on environmental management systems, ISO 14001, has propagated in this way down the supply chain, and labour standards such as SA8000 are becoming increasingly important for the same reason.

- *Discipline.* They often provide a systematic and disciplined way of operating in some area. It is always possible to develop an effective in-house way of doing things. But where standards provide a ready-made approach to follow, they can short-cut the work involved.

- *Learning and innovation.* The process of understanding and adopting a standard can be an important learning process for both individuals within an organisation and the organisation itself. The adoption of a standard can provide a new perspective with which to view the relevant business area, which can have unexpected spin-offs.

The disadvantages of standards are:

- *Obscure.* Standards are usually written to be precise. As a result they are often obscure documents that are difficult to understand. This will usually result in a few individuals within the organisation becoming experts and championing the standard.

- *Tick-box mentality.* The practice that standards suggest or prescribe is often rather bureaucratic and heavy on documentation. Attention can get diverted to following the checklist, rather than to promoting the behaviour (and spirit) that the standard intended.

- *Don't work.* It is not always clear that standards deliver what they say they will. Do environmental management system standards actually deliver better environmental performance, for example? There are cases where they do and cases where they don't. The jury, so far, is out.

....

CHAPTER 3

A Map of Standards

....

Standards Map

The map of standards shows some of the key relationships between different types of standard.

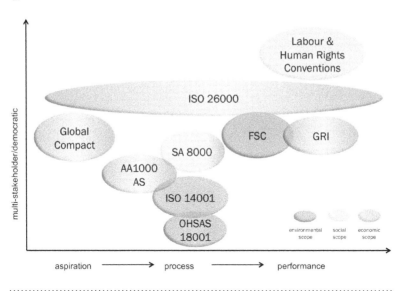

CHAPTER 4
Standards

THIS SECTION PRESENTS STANDARDS in four groups. The first group are the two 'fundamental standards' that underlie the social aspect of almost all other sustainability standards: human rights and labour rights. The second group consists of broad-ranging standards that cover all aspects of sustainability, typically at a high level only. The third group are those that directly address sustainability-related organisational practices, including their management and reporting. The fourth group are 'special purpose' standards. These address a particular issue or problem in more detail and may include aspects of labour rights together with corresponding management practices, for example.

Fundamental standards

Human rights

Background and purpose

Human rights are unlike most of the other standards in this book: they are not voluntary agreements between companies and stakeholders or even statutory regulations. Human rights derive from agreements between states. The seminal document is the Universal Declaration of Human Rights (UDHR) developed by the United Nations in 1948, which covered a range of issues including discrimination and property rights as well as political rights. The UDHR led to the International Covenant on Civil and Political Rights (ICCPR) and the International Covenant on Economic, Social and Cultural Rights (ICESCR) in the mid-1960s – and also to the European Convention on Human Rights in the 1950s. However, there are a great many human rights treaties and conventions dealing with particular human rights issues in detail.

The conventions, when they have been adopted and translated into national law, provide rights for citizens in relation to states; those states then have a duty to satisfy the rights. The conventions do not, directly, describe any specific obligations on companies.

The various human rights conventions are embodied and referred to by many of the other standards covered in this book, including ISO 26000, the Global Compact and the GRI.

Development and governance

The implementation of the human rights conventions is monitored by the UN Human Rights Council, composed of 47 members elected from UN member states, which reviews the human rights records of all member states.

It is important to note that a number of countries have not adopted various human rights conventions or parts of them. To date, the United States has not ratified the ICESCR and China has not ratified the ICCPR.

Nature of standard

There has been considerable debate between companies and civil society as to the applicability of human rights to companies. In 2011, after global consultations by Special UN Representative John Ruggie, the UN adopted the 'Guiding Principles on Business and Human Rights for implementing the UN "Protect, Respect and Remedy" Framework'.

The framework includes all human rights, including those labour rights defined in the Declaration on Fundamental Principles and Rights at Work, within the definition of human rights. It states that:

1. the state has a duty to protect human rights

2. companies have a duty to respect human rights

3. states should ensure that where human rights abuses occur, there are effective remedies available.

The standard in practice

The principles for implementation state that businesses should:

- avoid contributing directly or indirectly to human rights abuses

- develop human rights policies

- publicly state their commitment to respect human rights

- conduct due diligence assessments of their actual and potential human rights impacts and track the effectiveness of their responses to such impacts

- publicly report on how human rights are addressed, where risks of abuse are severe

- co-operate with state-based remediation

- establish their own grievance mechanisms available to all affected stakeholders.

Note that while human rights might appear to address only the social dimension of sustainability, some human rights instruments directly concern economic issues. In fact, all aspects of sustainability, including environmental issues can give rise to human rights issues and possibly abuses.

Websites.

http://www.ohchr.org/EN/Issues/Business/Pages/ SRSGTransCorpIndex.aspx

http://www2.ohchr.org/english/law/

....

Labour rights

Background and purpose

Labour rights, like human rights, are not agreements with individual companies directly. Labour rights result from the labour standards produced by the International Labour Organisation (ILO). The ILO is a tripartite body representing governments, workers and employers at an international level to promote 'decent work for all'. International labour standards are legal instruments drawn up by the ILO's three constituencies that set out basic principles and rights at work.

There are numerous ILO conventions and agreements of which eight are regarded as fundamental and are summarised in the Declaration on Fundamental Principles and Rights at Work.

Development and governance
International labour standards are developed through the ILO's tripartite structure. Employers and workers as well as governments are represented at every stage. However, to be effective, the conventions need to be incorporated into national law in each country. To date, neither the USA nor China has ratified all of the fundamental conventions.

Nature of standard
The eight fundamental principles cover the following six issues (some are covered by more than one):

- freedom of association

- the right to organise

- abolition of forced labour

- minimum working age

- elimination of child labour

- non-discrimination.

However, there are many other conventions covering numerous special circumstances, such as working conditions appropriate at sea or in agriculture, health and safety and non-discrimination at work.

The standard in practice

The ILO has also produced the Tripartite Declaration of Principles Concerning Multinational Enterprises and Social Policy, which give specific guidance to international companies. This covers issues such as respecting the sovereign rights of states, the treatment of workers in host countries, the generation and security of employment, training, wages and health and safety, amongst others.

International labour standards, while they do cover the issue of minimum wages, do not currently cover the issue of a 'living wage'.

International labour standards have been widely incorporated into a variety of sustainability standards that have been widely applied by companies. These include ISO 26000, SA 8000, GRI, ETI and Fair Labor, which are covered elsewhere in this guide. The ILO has been somewhat cautious in welcoming such derivative standards unless the active role of workers in monitoring their own conditions is sufficiently emphasised.

Websites.
http://www.ilo.org/global/standards/introduction-to-international-labour-standards/conventions-and-recommendations/lang–en/index.htm

http://www.ilo.org/empent/Publications/WCMS_094386/lang–en/index.htm

....

Broad spectrum standards

Global Compact: Sustainability aspiration

Background and purpose

The Global Compact was launched in 2000 in order 'to give a human face to globalisation'. It is primarily a set of aspirational principles supported by a large number of learning networks around the world.

In 2012, the Global Compact had some 8000 participants in 135 countries, of which 6000 are businesses. The local (country) networks are not financially supported by the UN.

Development and governance

The Global Compact is an initiative of the UN, led by the Secretary General's Office and supported by the Office of the High Commissioner for Human Rights (OHCHR), the International Labour Organization (ILO), the United Nations Environment Programme (UNEP), the United Nations Office on Drugs and Crime (UNODC), the United Nations Development Programme (UNDP), the United Nations Industrial Development Organization (UNIDO) and the United Nations Development Fund for Women (UNIFEM, part of UN Women). It therefore enjoys the legitimacy and authority of the UN.

While run by the UN Secretary General's Office, the compact maintains a multi-stakeholder advisory board, on which the stakeholder groups are business, civil society, labour and the United Nations.

Nature of standard

Adopting the Global Compact means that companies sign up to principles concerning:

- human rights

- avoiding complicity in human rights abuses

- freedom of association and collective bargaining

- the elimination of all forms of forced and compulsory labour

- the effective abolition of child labour

- the elimination of discrimination in respect of employment and occupation

- a precautionary approach to environmental challenges

- promotion of greater environmental responsibility

- the development and diffusion of environmentally friendly technologies

- anti-corruption.

Each year companies are also required to submit a report on their progress in relation to the ten principles, including a statement of support from their chief executive. These 'communications on progress' (COPs) are published on the Global Compact website. While there is no check on the quality of the COPs, repeated failure to submit a COP can lead to expulsion from the Global Compact. A GRI report is recommended by the Global Compact as a good vehicle for preparing a COP.

The standard in practice

The Global Compact has the largest membership of any corporate responsibility organisation. The compact also has an extensive presence in the non-developed world, one of the few corporate responsibility organisations to do so. The Global Compact has done much to legitimise the consideration by companies of human rights and the other issues covered by its principles.

Most of the activity of the Global Compact takes place within the national or regional learning networks, which regularly hold meetings and conferences.

The Global Compact recognises three levels of adherence to the principles and disclosure (COPs): learner, active and advanced.

Website
http://www.unglobalcompact.org/index.html

Case study: The Global Compact and corruption

Novozymes is a Danish multinational biotech company working on enzymes and micro-organisms. The company's products are manufactured on most continents and sold worldwide. Novozymes signed the Global Compact in 2002.

Novozymes manages its sustainability systematically across the company at Vice-President level. Corruption is handled by a committee on Business Integrity. Executive management bonuses depend in part on corporate responsibility performance. The company publishes an integrated online annual report that includes its Global Compact Communication on Progress. Novozymes was also a member of the Global Compact Working Group on the 10th Principle (anti-corruption).

Novozymes has developed a management standard that all employees must comply with. This has six principles:

- *Bribes.* We do not give or accept bribes.

- *Facilitation payments.* We pay only reluctantly to expedite public services.

- *Money laundering.* We do not assist in laundering money from criminal activities.

- *Protection money.* We do not pay criminals for protection.

- *Gifts.* We do not give or receive big gifts.

- *Political and charitable contributions.* We do not give money to political parties but sometimes we contribute to charities.

The company has established mechanisms for employees to:

1. Seek guidance from senior finance directors when unclear on a particular course of action.

2. Raise concerns anonymously on the company intranet or with the General Counsel.

3. Report facilitation payments and large gifts.

The development of the business integrity measures took a year overseen by a cross-functional group. Particular attention was paid to clarifying how the management standard should be applied in different countries. It is regarded as under continual development.

Novozymes anti-corruption measures were developed as a response to numerous pressures, including customer demand, the assessments for ethical investment funds, the requirements of the Sarbanes-Oxley Act in the USA, compliance with Danish law, preparing for future legislation and facilitating company audits. Securing competitive advantage and managing risk were both important.

SOURCE: Global Compact. 2006. *Business against Corruption* (New York: Global Compact).

OECD Guidelines for Multinational Enterprises

Background and purpose

The OECD is an international membership organisation for states. Its members are mainly, but not entirely, developed nations. Its purpose is to promote economic development. The OECD maintains two standing stakeholder committees: the trade union advisory committee and the business and industry advisory committee.

The OECD has produced a number of different guidelines relevant to large companies including:

- bribery in international business transactions

- corporate governance

- multinational enterprises.

This section concentrates on the OECD Guidelines for Multinational Enterprises, but the other guidelines listed above are also relevant standards for sustainability.

Development and governance

The OECD Guidelines for Multinational Enterprises were first published in 1976. They are part of the OECD's Declaration on International Investment and Multinational Enterprises and were last revised in 2011.

The OECD Guidelines for Multinational Enterprises are intended to provide guidance only. Nevertheless, they are unique in that they are supported by a monitoring mechanism. Governments that adhere to the guidelines (i.e. all OECD members together with other governments that declare their adherence to the guidelines) are required to establish a National Contact Point (NCP). This may be an individual or a body of people drawn from various backgrounds. The NCPs are mandated to handle complaints about specific instances of company misconduct in relation to the guidelines. NCPs will work through mediation, but can also make public determinations that the guidelines have been breached.

Nature of standard

The guidelines cover the following issues:

- disclosure
- human rights
- employment and industrial relations
- the environment
- combating bribery
- consumer interests
- science and technology

- competition

- taxation.

Overall, the guidelines provide advice consistent with the other standards covered in this book. They have been written to be consistent with UN guidance on human rights. However, they go beyond most other sustainability standards in their coverage of science and technology, competition and taxation. In respect of science and technology their aim is to promote diffusion. In relation to competition, the guidelines advocate avoiding all anti-competitive activities. In relation to tax the advice is to apply the spirit, rather than only the letter, of relevant laws, for example in conforming to arm's length transfer pricing practices.

The standard in practice

Due to the membership of the OECD, the guidelines in theory apply to a large proportion of some of the most significant companies in the world. However, the number of companies that explicitly use them for guidance is unknown.

What is known is the number of 'specific instances' (i.e. potential breaches) that have been considered through the NCP mechanism. In the years from 2000 to June 2011, 262 instances were raised, with 39 new ones in the year to June 2011 (more than double the number raised in the previous year).

Website

http://www.oecd.org/daf/internationalinvestment/
guidelinesformultinationalenterprises/

Case study: Vedanta and the OECD

Final Statement by the UK National Contact Point for the OECD Guidelines for Multinational Enterprises (September 2009):

Complaint from Survival International against Vedanta Resources plc

Summary of the Conclusions

The UK National Contact Point (NCP) for the OECD Guidelines for Multinational Enterprises (the Guidelines) upholds Survival International's allegation that Vedanta Resources plc (Vedanta) has not complied with Chapter V(2)(b) of the Guidelines. The UK NCP concludes that Vedanta failed to put in place an adequate and timely consultation mechanism fully to engage the Dongria Kondh, an indigenous community who would be directly affected by the environmental and health and safety impact of its plans to construct a bauxite mine in the Niyamgiri Hills, Orissa, India.

The UK NCP upholds Survival International's allegation that Vedanta has not complied with Chapter II(7) of the Guidelines. It concludes that Vedanta failed to engage the Dongria Kondh in adequate and timely consultations about the construction of the mine, or to use other mechanisms to assess the implications of its activities on the community such as an indigenous or human rights impact assessment. Vedanta therefore failed to develop and apply effective self-regulatory practices to foster a relationship of confidence and mutual trust between the company and an important constituent of the society in which it was operating.

The UK NCP also upholds Survival International's allegation that Vedanta has not behaved consistently with Chapter II(2) of the Guidelines. The UK NCP concludes that Vedanta failed to engage the Dongria Kondh in adequate and timely consultations on the construction of the bauxite mine; it did not consider the impact of the construction of the mine on the rights and freedoms of the Dongria Kondh, or balance the impact against the need to promote the success of the company. For these reasons, Vedanta did not respect the rights and freedoms of the Dongria Kondh consistent with India's commitments under various international human rights instruments, including the UN International Covenant on Civil and Political Rights, the UN Convention on the Elimination of All Forms of Racial Discrimination, the Convention on Biological Diversity and the UN Declaration on the Rights of Indigenous People.

SOURCE: www.oecd.org/dataoecd/49/16/43884129.pdf Similar

Organisational practice standards

AA1000: Report assurance

Background and purpose

The term 'AA1000' actually refers to a family of standards:

- AA1000 APS contains the accountability principles that apply to the other two standards in the family.

- AA1000 SES is a standard for stakeholder engagement designed to ensure good practice is followed.

- AA1000 AS is a standard for assurance of sustainability reports designed to support their credibility.

Development and governance

The AA1000 standards were originally developed in the late 1990s by an inclusive multi-stakeholder group. The original standard contained elements of all three of the current versions. Subsequent versions were developed in the same spirit by the Institute for Social and Ethical Accountability (ISEA), a not-for-profit organisation. ISEA later changed its name to 'AccountAbility'. More recently, AccountAbility became a consultancy although the development of the standards has been delegated to a Community Interest Company. The nature of the continued governance of the standards is less clear.

AccountAbility also developed a training and accreditation infrastructure associated with the assurance standard. This is intended to ensure that accredited assurance practitioners apply the standard in a consistent way.

Nature of standard

AA1000 APS (2008) describes three principles of accountability:

- *Inclusivity.* This concerns the participation of stakeholders in accountability-related processes, including reporting, assurance and stakeholder engagement.

- *Materiality.* This concerns the necessity, from an accountability perspective, of dealing with those issues that are important to stakeholders.

- *Responsiveness.* This concerns responding to stakeholder needs and interests through reporting and engagement.

AA1000 SES (2011) is a guidance standard for good practice in engaging stakeholders. It is based on the three principles of accountability above and contains three parts that set out how to:

- establish commitment to stakeholder engagement

- define the purpose, scope and stakeholders within an engagement process

- recognise good quality engagements.

AA1000 AS (2008) defines two types of assurance engagement. Type 1 is designed to provide assurance that an organisation's report adheres to the accountability principles. Type 2 provides assurance over the organisation's sustainability performance as well as the principles. The standard also distinguishes two levels of assurance: moderate and high. These levels are designed to reflect the level of confidence that the assurance provider, and hence stakeholders, can feel in the assurance statement. This will be affected not only by the quality of the report but also the effort that underpins the assurance process. The standard also sets out:

- how the assurance engagement process should be conducted

- the overall format of the assurance statement

- the necessary competencies of the assurance provider.

The standard in practice

AA1000 SES has been used to provide guidance on stakeholder engagement. It is a useful safeguard against the use of the term 'stakeholder engagement' to refer to one-way communications exercises that do not include stakeholder participation.

AA1000 AS is one of only two standards that are used to provide sustainability report assurance. The other is ISAE 3000, which is the standard that financial accountants are required to use for the assurance of non-financial information. The chief differences between AA1000 AS and ISAE 3000 are that the latter is confined to ascertaining the correctness of information and also that the content of the assurance provider's statement is more limited.

AA1000 AS has been used for the assurance of approaching 200 reports each year. The organisations that use the standard range from large multinationals to SMEs, including some social enterprises. It is common to use the standard to provide assurance for GRI reports.

Website
http://www.accountability.org/standards/

Case study: Assurance statement

The assurance process culminates in the production of a written statement providing feedback to the company and stakeholders and is included in the report being assured. The following is extracted from Vodafone's 2011 sustainability report assurance statement.

We saw that Vodafone engages with government, consumers and NGO stakeholders at both Group and local levels. There are processes in place across the organisation to engage and learn from stakeholder feedback. During the year significant disruption occurred in a number of markets notably in the Middle East. Vodafone will need to review whether its approach to stakeholder engagement and responsiveness is sufficient to balance stakeholder needs and define appropriate responses in these rapidly changing markets.

Vodafone Group's guidelines for reporting environmental data have been disseminated to all the markets. However, during our local market visits we noted that the internal review of sustainability data in certain markets could be improved to help build confidence in the data sets used to manage these issues.

Vodafone consistently reports against its objectives many of which are qualitative in nature and are set on a short-term basis. We saw evidence of a number of strategic initiatives which could shape Vodafone's sustainability direction over a number of years. Vodafone could consider including a roadmap of its sustainability journey over the next few years to enable stakeholders to assess progress over a longer period of time.

SOURCE: http://www.vodafone.com/content/index/about/sustainability/ sustainability_vision.html

GRI: Reporting

Background and purpose

The GRI (Global Reporting Initiative) is a standard for sustainability reports. Its aim is to ensure reasonable comprehensiveness and consistency between sustainability reports

Development and governance

The standard was originally produced by a broad multi-stakeholder group with significant public consultation across the world. Its continuing development is supported by a formal multi-stakeholder governance structure. The GRI is a not-for-profit organisation based in Amsterdam.

The first draft standard was produced in 1999 with the first definitive version launched in 2000. The GRI is being continually revised and developed. The fourth generation of the standard, G4, will probably be launched in 2013.

Nature of standard

The GRI is a set of guidelines for sustainability reporting. This includes:

- A set of *principles* that should govern sustainability reporting, such as the inclusion of stakeholders and the clarity of data reported.

- A list of *indicators* that identify the information that should be reported.

- A set of *protocols* that define how the data underlying each indicator should be compiled and presented.

- *Sector-specific guidelines* for certain industry sectors, such as the automotive industry and the food processing industry. These typically build on the general guidelines.

- A few *national annexes* that tailor the general guidelines to take account of particular national concerns.

The full set of indicators covers social, economic and environmental issues. The principal categories are:

- economic

- environmental

- human rights

- labour practices

- product responsibility

- society.

Some indicators are quantitative and performance-based while others refer to the management systems relating to particular issues. The indicators are divided into core and additional indicators. There are nearly 80 performance indicators of which about 50 are 'core'.

It is demanding to report on all of the indicators and it is recognised that companies may start by reporting on a smaller set and increase the number of indicators reported over time. Up to the third generation of the guidelines, the GRI provided a formal way that companies could declare the extent to which they had reported on the full indicator set.

GRI reports do not require auditing. The GRI, however, provides for auditing and has in the past recognised this in recommended formats for companies' self-declarations.

The standard in practice

The GRI is increasingly referred to in national regulation as a good model for sustainability reporting. There are no significant alternatives to the GRI for general sustainability reporting. However, with a new initiative focusing on 'integrated reporting', the International Integrated Reporting Council (IIRC) is beginning to look at how regulated annual financial reports might integrate sustainability reporting.

Technically, the GRI is applicable to all organisations, but in practice the large majority of GRI reports have been produced by companies. In 2010 nearly 2000 organisations reported using the GRI guidelines.

Website

https://www.globalreporting.org

Case study: Reporting

EMC is a large, US-based company providing information infrastructure and virtual infrastructure technologies. It has more than 53,000 employees. Since 2007, EMC has supplemented its US Securities and Exchange Commission (SEC) filings with a sustainability report on its activities. They use the Global Reporting Initiative framework, a standard that is, in their opinion 'to sustainability reporting what Generally Accepted Accounting Principles (and their global companion, International Financial Reporting Standards) are to financial reporting'.

EMC uses the GRI framework to follow a process of identifying relevant and material topics on which they should report. GRI provides a useful checklist that can be adapted and tailored by individual companies – it is not a check-the-box reporting exercise. Currently, EMC do not have their sustainability report audited.

Consistent with the GRI framework, EMC focuses its reporting on topics that are important to their business under the three categories of environmental, social and economic. Each category has a series of detailed indicators that EMC uses to determine the topics most significant to their business. They also seek input from their shareholders, customers, employees and suppliers, and obtain information from structured analyses of their sustainability impacts, dependencies and opportunities. Each year they review the GRI indicators and consider where they can and should expand the scope of their reporting.

....

SOURCE: http://www.directorship.com/sustainability-and-the-board-the-emc-story/

ISO 14001: Environmental management

Background and purpose

ISO is an international membership organisation. Its members are national standards bodies from almost every country in the world. The most active participants in national standards bodies and in ISO are primarily companies. However, consumers also have a formal place in the governance of ISO and the development of many of its standards.

ISO 14001 is one of the ISO 14000 series of standards concerning various aspects of environmental issues. ISO 14001 is a standard for environmental management systems. It is intended to ensure that environmental management systems are implemented in a systematic and effective manner.

Development and governance

ISO 14001 was developed within the ISO structure taking British Standard BS 7750 as its template. The development process made some allowance for a wider range of stakeholders than might be normal in an ISO development. All ISO standards are subject to review every three to five years.

Nature of standard

ISO 14001 (2004) is based on the plan-do-check-act model, designed to ensure that:

- The objectives of environmental management are clear and the required processes are identified (*plan*).

- The processes are implemented (*do*).

- The resulting performance is monitored (*check*).

- A review is undertaken of the effectiveness of the system (*act*).

The standard is built around the idea of *continual improvement* of the management system. It includes attention to the structure of the management system, resources and roles, training and competencies, communications and the establishment of an aspects register for the organisation.

The standard includes requirements against which conformance can be formally assessed. It also includes guidance on the implementation of the standard. An organisation may claim conformity with the standard or arrange for external parties to verify that conformity.

The standard in practice

ISO 14001 is one of the most widely used ISO standards (after ISO 9001, the quality management system standard) and certainly the most widely implemented environmental management system standard. There have been over 100,000 implementations of ISO 14001.

ISO 14001 is similar to the European Commission-sponsored EMAS scheme. The development of the two standards appears to be converging. EMAS now effectively includes ISO 14001.

While there is no doubt that ISO 14001 will result in a systematic management system, the effectiveness of such systems in improving environmental performance has been questioned.

The structure of ISO 14001 is similar to that of ISO 9001. It is not uncommon for companies implementing both standards to combine the management processes involved.

Website

http://www.iso.org/iso/home/store/catalogue_tc/catalogue_detail. htm?csnumber=31807

Case study: ISO 14001 in practice

Permadoor makes plastic doors, largely for the social housing market. Due to customer demand and the rising cost of resources, including electricity and waste disposal, the company was interested in introducing an environmental management system. ISO 14001 was chosen.

Following a review of the site and current practices and external advice on identifying and prioritising environmental aspects and impacts, an environmental management plan was developed. The plan included new approaches to waste handling, energy monitoring and paper use.

The new ISO 14001 systems were integrated with existing quality and health and safety management systems.

ISO 14001 certification was achieved at one site in 2006. Further plans include the introduction of the standard to the company's other sites and further attention to recycling rates.

SOURCE: www.eco.uk.com/downloads/casestudy-permadoor.pdf

ISO 26000: Social responsibility

Background and purpose

ISO 26000 is a standard for social responsibility. It was designed to be applicable to any kind of organisations, from companies to non-governmental organisations (NGOs) and those from the public sector.

ISO 26000 defines 'social responsibility' as the:

- responsibility of an organisation for the impacts of its decisions and activities on society and the environment, through transparent and ethical behaviour that:

  - contributes to sustainable development, including health and the welfare of society
  - takes into account the expectations of stakeholders
  - is in compliance with applicable law and consistent with international norms of behaviour and
  - is integrated throughout the organisation and practised in its relationships.

Development and governance

ISO 26000 was developed over a period of almost eight years and published in 2010. The standard was developed by a Working Group designed with a stakeholder structure that was enforced wherever possible. This allocated each expert delegate participating in its development to one of six categories:

- industry

- government

- consumer

- NGO

- labour

- 'SSRO', which covered all other types of stakeholder.

Real efforts were made to balance representation from the developing world as well as the developed world. The chair was from Brazil while the co-chair was from Sweden. The ISO 26000 Working Group, as a result, was the first ISO standard to have more representation from developing countries than from developed ones. The attempt to reach balance also extended to each of the many sub-working groups during the development of the standard.

In order to ensure consistency of interpretation with other major standards and initiatives, ISO drew up Memoranda of Understanding with the ILO, the Global Compact (which is often described as the largest CSR initiative in the world) and with the OECD. This means that ISO 26000 is nowhere contrary to the intent of the Global Compact, the OECD Guidelines or the ILO Conventions. The consistency with ILO Conventions means that it is also broadly compatible with other standards derived from them, such as SA 8000 and the ETI.

All ISO standards are subject to review every three to five years.

Nature of standard

ISO 26000 is a guidance standard, not a certifiable standard. It is also not a management system standard. For those who have worked with ISO 14001, this is unfamiliar territory. However, within the overall ISO portfolio of standards, it is not unusual.

The structure of the main part of the standard covers:

- principles of social responsibility

- recognition of social responsibility and engaging with stakeholders

- seven core subjects:
  - organisational governance
  - human rights
  - labour practices
  - the environment
  - fair operating practices
  - consumer issues
  - community involvement and development

- integrating social responsibility within an organisation.

Between them the core subjects define some 37 more detailed issues. These include matters such as governance, human rights risk situations, health and safety at work, prevention of pollution, anti-corruption, sustainable consumption and technology development and access. This represents one of the most extensive lists of sustainability issues for a company.

The section on integrating social responsibility describes management practices related to social responsibility such as communication and the need to identify relevant and significant issues and dealing practically with the organisation's sphere of influence.

The standard in practice

ISO 26000 has achieved considerable awareness globally. It has been influential at policy level in the EU and has altered the way ISO develops standards towards a more stakeholder-inclusive approach.

ISO 26000 appears to have been particularly influential with Asian and Latin American companies. Because it is not a certifiable standard, it is not possible to count the number of companies that have made use of it. Nevertheless, during 2011 ISO 26000 was one of the top-selling ISO standards.

Some companies have extended their implementation of the ISO 14001 standard by capturing within the ISO 14001 aspects register a wider set sustainability issues (including social and economic ones) drawn from ISO 26000.

Website

http://www.iso.org/iso/home/standards/iso26000.htm

Case study: ISO 26000

Step Ahead AG is a small German software company employing about 40 people, including part-time staff. Their software supports business and management functions, particularly of small and medium enterprises.

Step Ahead AG states that:

we use ISO 26000 for our orientation and integrate its recommendations into our values and practices. We consider it a useful instrument to identify issues where our small company can reasonably contribute to the development of society.

Since Germany is a highly regulated country we have first of all to take into account all relevant laws and regulations in regard of society, the environment, health and safety at the workplace etc.

The issues identified are:

* *human development and training in the workplace*

* *prevention of pollution*

* *sustainable resource use*

* *education and culture*

* *employment creation and skills development, and*

* *social investment.*

We are ready to share our deliberations and findings with those interested and particularly with our suppliers and customers.

SOURCE: http://www.26k-estimation.com/html/good_iso_26000_examples.html#stepahead

Special purpose standards

Fairtrade: Producers

Background and purpose

The purpose of Fairtrade standards is to support producers in the developing world to enable them to enjoy decent livelihoods. There are numerous Fairtrade standards relating to different products and the nature of the producer.

Fairtrade standards in general provide for:

- a minimum price

- a premium above market rates

- minimum working conditions

- environmental standards

- the provision of support for producers to develop their business.

Fairtrade standards also provide for a consumer-facing label identifying products as being fairtrade.

Development and governance

The first Fairtrade initiatives were established in the 1980s. The Dutch 'Max Havellar' brand for coffee is credited with being the first full Fairtrade scheme.

Unlike most other standards which are developed from a single vision top-down, Fairtrade is the result of a number of separate schemes joining together. As a result of that, and of the scale of the businesses involved today, its structure is fairly complex.

In 1997 Fairtrade Labelling Organizations International (FLO) was established. FLO manages the standards and their development. The certification of products, which is necessary if they carry the label, is supervised by FLO-CERT which inspects and certifies producer organisations and also audits intermediary traders.

FLO has 25 members that produce or promote Fairtrade products. These include licensing organisations, some marketing organisations and three producer groups. The governance of the members varies, but various stakeholder groups can be involved. In the UK the member is the Fairtrade Foundation, which is a charity founded by CAFOD, Christian Aid, Oxfam, Traidcraft, the World Development Movement and the National Federation of Women's Institutes.

Nature of standard

Fairtrade standards cover producer organisations of varying types and companies that trade Fairtrade products.

Fairtrade standards vary by product. Most Fairtrade products are food and drinks, such as sugar, coffee and tea. However, more recently products such as gold, charcoal and rubber gloves have gained certification.

A typical Fairtrade standard will provide for:

- traceability

- labelling, packaging and product description

- management of production practices

- environmental protection

- labour conditions

- producer financing

- minimum prices

- premium pricing

- producer support.

The standard in practice

In 2012 Fairtrade standards covered over 300 raw products alone. The six biggest Fairtrade products were bananas, cocoa, coffee, cotton, sugar and tea. Total Fairtrade sales were nearly 5 billion euros. The standards also covered 1.2m workers in 66 countries and nearly 1000 producer organisations. This resulted in about 65m euros of premium paid to producers.

Website
http://www.fairtrade.net

Case study: Poverty and Fairtrade
The Traidcraft approach to poverty:

Working to eradicate child labour is clearly an important process. Child labour is both a cause and an effect of poverty, in a reinforcing cycle. When children work instead of being educated, their chances as an adult of getting a better job or being able to press for their rights as workers are minimal. Children's work also replaces the need to pay an adult, so increasing poverty in the older generations. If the adults in a family cannot earn enough by their work, children's labour will be needed to help feed and clothe them. So initiatives which help workers to organise for better pay and other rights are important to break the cycle of poverty. If adults – especially women – are paid fairly for their work, children will benefit through being able to afford to go to school.

However, until fairer conditions have been established, it may be unrealistic or even undesirable to expect children not to be involved in economic processes. In situations of extreme poverty, everyone needs to work to survive – and education may not be available as an alternative for children. The impact of HIV/Aids can mean that in some families parents are unable to work and children need to work to support their parents and younger siblings.

Even in less extreme situations, it is important to distinguish between children working in ways which can bring benefits and enforced child labour, which can affect their health and development and exclude children from educational opportunities. Much craft work, for example, is home-based or undertaken in small family-run workshops. In these *circumstances helping out part-time, alongside attending schools, is often a normal part of growing up.*

In many cases this is a way for youngsters to learn traditional skills which will help provide them with an income as adults. So abolishing children's work completely may even have negative effects. For example, one of our suppliers, Tara Projects in India, sells products sourced from a number of different craft producers. Initially Tara advised their producers against any work by children. However, this led to some children starting to look down on their parents' craft, and Tara realised that as well as getting schooling, children should be encouraged to learn craft skills that would increase their job prospects. At the same time they should also grow up aware of how to protect their interests better than previous generations had been able to do.

Similarly, small-scale farmers will often involve all family members at busy times like harvest, and parents will want to pass on agricultural skills to their children.

SOURCE: http://www.traidcraft.co.uk/publications_and_resources/traidcraft_publications/factsheets.htm

FSC: Wood

Background and purpose

The Forest Stewardship Council (FSC) standard is a system for promoting sustainable forestry products. It provides a label on consumer products that certifies that the product has been sourced from a sustainable forest.

The FSC standard is a product-based standard, rather than an organisational standard. Standards similar to the FSC include the Marine Stewardship Council and the Aquaculture Stewardship Council.

Development and governance

The FSC was formed in the early 1990s by a multi-stakeholder group, including timber users, traders and representatives of environmental and human rights organisations.

The FSC is a member-controlled organisation run by a stakeholder council split into three chambers: environmental, social and economic. Each chamber has equal voting power and within each chamber votes are weighted so that representatives from the global South have equal weight to those from the global North.

Nature of standard

The FSC standard has two main components:

- A set of requirements for forests to be designated sustainable. These are mainly environmental, social and economic performance requirements; however, there are also some management requirements.

- A set of requirements for the chain of custody, or traceability, of wood and products manufactured from it. These specify the nature of the management system that must be employed for certifiable products.

In addition, retail consumer products made from wood traceable back to a sustainable source can be labelled with an FSC logo that consumers can recognise.

The forest sustainability requirements are derived from ten principles:

- Compliance with laws and FSC Principles – to comply with all laws, regulations, treaties, conventions and agreements, together with all FSC Principles and Criteria.

- Tenure and use rights and responsibilities – to define, document and legally establish long-term tenure and use rights.

- Indigenous peoples' rights – to identify and uphold indigenous peoples' rights of ownership and use of land and resources.

- Community relations and workers' rights – to maintain or enhance forest workers' and local communities' social and economic well-being.

- Benefits from the forest – to maintain or enhance long-term economic, social and environmental benefits from the forest.

- Environmental impact – to maintain or restore the ecosystem, its biodiversity, resources and landscapes.

- Management plan – to have a management plan, implemented, monitored and documented.

- Monitoring and assessment – to demonstrate progress towards management objectives.

- Maintenance of high conservation value forests – to maintain or enhance the attributes which define such forests.

- Plantations – to plan and manage plantations in accordance with FSC Principles and Criteria.

The FSC does not provide certification services, which may be purchased from commercial certifiers. However, the FSC does require that certifiers have been accredited with the FSC. There are two main types of certification: for forest management and for the chain of custody.

The standard in practice

The FSC standard covers over 162m ha of forests across all continents. Most of this is publicly owned land.

The standard requires that not only the originating forest, but each facility that handles wood from the forest, throughout the chain of custody, must be certified as having adequate management systems. This ensures confidence that wood from sustainable sources can be fully traced and that it is not mixed with wood from other sources.

Over 1100 forest certificates and some 23,000 chain of custody certificates had been issued by mid-2012.

Implementing the FSC standard is relatively demanding. However, the resulting rigour ensures that the standard is widely trusted. Its implementation is growing steadily.

Website

http://www.fsc.org

Case study: FSC in Portugal

Prompted by demand from their suppliers, a group of four cork farmers in Portugal decided in 2006 to work together to gain FSC certification. Cork is produced by the bark of the cork oak, which is harvested once every nine years. Cork oak farming is therefore able to co-exist with other low-intensity uses of the land.

From a sustainability perspective it was not initially clear how cork farming could be best managed. There was also a lack of knowledge of threatened species on their land. The cork farmers worked with WWF to ascertain how much land should be set aside from farming. From a management perspective the farmers' management practices were not documented. Working collectively enabled them to commission appropriate training.

Today the cork farmers' association has grown to include 300 members and a forested area of 174,000 ha. The biodiversity of the montado region of Portugal has been protected. FSC certified cork products enjoy a market premium over non-certified products.

SOURCE: http://www.pre.fsc.org/casestudies.html

PRI: Investment

Background and purpose

The PRI is designed to encourage attention to environmental, social and governance (ESG) issues in investment decision-making. It is aimed at mainstream investors as well as 'socially responsible investors'.

Development and governance

The United Nations Principles for Responsible Investment (PRI) was an initiative of the UN Secretary General in 2005.

The PRI was initially drafted by a group of investors in 2005, supported by a multi-stakeholder advisory group. The drafting process was coordinated by the United Nations Environment Programme Finance Initiative (UNEP FI) and the UN Global Compact (UNGC). They were launched in 2006.

The PRI now is supported by UNEP FI and UNGC. It is governed by an Advisory Council of which the majority of members are asset owners. Other members include two UN representatives and four investment managers or service providers. About a third of seats are reserved for asset owners from major regions of the world, to ensure there is a reasonable geographic representation.

Nature of standard

Investor organisations can become members of the PRI, committed to upholding the Principles. The PRI contains six Principles covering a commitment to:

- the incorporation of ESG issues into investment analysis and decision-making

- active ownership and the incorporation of ESG issues into ownership policies

- make disclosures on ESG issues by the entities invested in

- promote the acceptance and implementation of the Principles within the investment industry

- co-operative working between members of the PRI

- report on activities and progress towards implementing the Principles.

Each Principle is supported by a list of 'possible actions' that its members are can take. These are in effect more detailed recommendations on how to implement the Principles. They cover matters such as:

- encouraging academic research on responsible investment

- the development of ESG-related metrics

- engagement with investee companies

- the promotion of the GRI for their reporting

- disclosure on how the Principles are being implemented.

The standard in practice

The PRI now has over 1100 signatories of whom nearly 700 are investment managers, with about a third as many asset owners and fewer than 200 service providers. The large majority of members are from the developed world. Their number includes some of the largest asset owners in the world, such as CalPERS, the California state employees' pension fund.

The PRI publishes regular annual reports providing full details of its survey of members and how they are implementing the Principles. This includes details of the funds covered and the way ESG issues are integrated into the operation of the signatory.

Website

http://www.unpri.org

....

SA8000: Supply chain

Background and purpose

SA8000 includes both performance requirements and management system requirements and is a verifiable standard for workplace conditions and their management. It is applicable to any organisation.

Development and governance

In the mid-1990s the Council on Economic Priorities convened a multi-stakeholder Advisory Board to develop standards for the workplace. This included businesses, unions, socially responsible investors, government and NGOs. The non-profit organisation Social Accountability International (SAI) was formed in 1996 to develop the standard SA8000. SA8000 is a standard for workplace conditions. SAI also delivers training programmes connected with the standard. An accreditation programme for verifiers was also developed but separated from SAI in 2007 to form a separate organisation Social Accountability Accreditation Services (SAAS).

Nature of standard

The standard includes high-level requirements for 'social accountability' which cover:

- child labour

- forced and compulsory labour

- health and safety

- freedom of association and collective bargaining

- discrimination

- disciplinary practices

- working hours

- remuneration.

It also includes requirements for management systems that cover:

- policies for labour conditions

- manager and worker representation

- the management cycle for labour conditions, covering review, planning and implementation

- control of sub-contractors and suppliers, requiring the imposition of SA8000 on the supply chain

- corrective action

- communication with stakeholders.

The standard provides for the certification of specific sites. Certification is undertaken by assurance providers that have been accredited by SAAS.

The standard in practice

SA8000 has been successful. There are over 2000 certified sites that together employ over 1m workers.

One key to its success has been the requirement on an organisation seeking certification to impose the standard on its suppliers. This leads to a propagation of the standard throughout supply chains.

The sectors that have been particularly active in adopting SA8000 include shoes and clothing, toys and agriculture. These are sectors with significant Western demand supplied through labour in the developing world and where there have been serious concerns about the treatment of workers.

Websites.
http://www.sa-intl.org/index.cfm?fuseaction=Page.ViewPage&pageId=937

http://www.saasaccreditation.org/

Case study: SA8000 and the Global Compact
Sabaf is an Italian manufacturer of components for domestic cooking appliances with about 700 employees. In 2003 the company developed its Charter of Values, drawing on human rights and elements of SA8000. It joined the Global Compact in 2004 and pursued SA8000 certification in 2005. It also uses the AA1000 SES standard to guide their stakeholder engagement practices.

SA8000 certification does not currently extend to its subsidiaries, although policies guaranteeing compliance to SA8000 are implemented within them and the eventual goal is full certification. While the implementation of SA8000 in Italy was straightforward, implementing it in its newer operations in Brazil was more challenging, with difficulty in finding appropriate staff to manage the process.

The implementation of SA800 is seen as a way of putting the Global Compact principles into practice. The standards also help to institutionalise Sabaf's values and communicate them to stakeholders.

Sabaf finds its customers' purchasing decisions still start with price, even when the customer is also a member of the Global Compact. However, as a result of its active implementation of standards, there is a high level of awareness of its commitment to social and environmental performance amongst its customers. The CEO also believes that the use of ethical standards is reflected in favourable investor attitudes and in the company's stock price.

SOURCE: http://www.sa-intl.org/index.cfm?fuseaction=Page.ViewPage& PageID=1012

Voluntary Principles: Security

Background and purpose

The Voluntary Principles are designed to apply to companies in the extractive sectors, i.e. mining, oil and gas. They elaborate on expectations of companies in establishing security for their facilities consistent with the human rights of local communities.

Development and governance

The Voluntary Principles were developed by the US and UK governments in a forum in 2000 that brought them together with human rights NGOs and responsible business organisations. At the end of that year the principles were agreed and published.

While the number of participants (especially companies) in the Voluntary Principles has grown, the principles themselves have not been subsequently revised although additional guidance in the form of 'tools' has been developed.

Nature of standard

The Voluntary Principles are guidance only. There is no monitoring of their application. They cover three areas:

- risk assessment

- company relations with public security

- company relations with private security.

Risk assessment suggests that companies, in reviewing human rights risks in a particular location, should consider amongst other factors:

- the potential for violence

- the record of the public security forces, government law enforcement and private security forces

- the capacity of the judiciary to hold people to account for human rights abuses.

The standard recommends that company relations with host government's public security should include regular talks on human rights issues, the impact of security arrangements and the company's ethical policies. It should also cover detailed issues such as the reporting of violent incidents, responses to human rights abuses and arms trading regulation.

Private security forces should be engaged only if public security is likely to be inadequate. Company relations with private security companies should ensure, amongst other things, that they only provide defensive capability, any allegations of abuse are recorded and that the right of freedom of association should not be impeded.

The standard also recommends that the UN Principles on the Use of Force and Firearms by Law Enforcement Officials and the UN Code of Conduct for Law Enforcement Officials should be applied by public and private security forces alike.

The standard in practice

The Voluntary Principles have been very influential in companies' responses to human rights abuses. However, it is difficult to know what effect the Voluntary Principles have actually had on the ground as there is no public reporting or auditing of its use.

Website

http://www.voluntaryprinciples.org/
....

CHAPTER 5

Decision time

···

Which standard will do what I want?

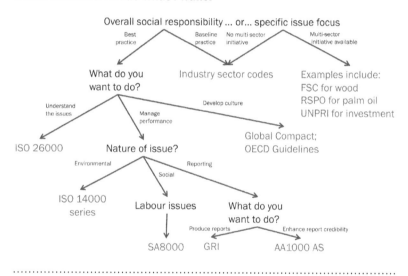

Overall social responsibility ... or... specific issue focus

···

CHAPTER 6

Putting Standards into Practice

USING STANDARDS WITHIN AN ORGANISATION is a demanding experience. The standards themselves can be complex and hard to understand. Often they are not written with a view to their implementation and guidance may be lacking. And to cap it all, the reaction from those affected may well be on the lines of 'not another one!'

This guide does not pretend to be a complete guide to all the different types of standards that have been described, still less a guide to all those that have not been covered. What this final section does is to pull out some key lessons that may be useful to those considering getting involved with a sustainability standard.

Get involved before the standard even exists!

If you are aware that a standard is being developed in an area that is relevant and important for your organisation, then get involved in that development. At the least, this will mean that you will gain a deeper understanding of what the standard is trying to do. But it may also enable you to shape the development of the standard, so that it is more practical or useful or effective in some way.

Of course, standards development is rarely a single time process. Standards are regularly revised and so it may be possible to get involved in the review and re-development of a standard. That will bring many of the benefits of working on the original development of the standard. However, working on the initial development of a standard, or on its revision, takes time and that needs to be taken into account in any decision to participate.

Use the standard implementation process as an awareness-raising exercise

Too often implementing a standard can be resented: it takes time and effort and may require new processes or possibly forms to fill in. There may be no getting away from some of that, but that doesn't have to be how staff encounter the standard or how it is presented. A sustainability standard will be concerned with 'raising standards' in some area that most people will value, be it a clean environment or human rights. Many will value some time to appreciate the real issues involved and actually be quite keen to do something to help improve the situation.

Moreover, it is not only those who will be involved at a day-to-day level that might be approached. Senior management and board members should be included in an awareness-raising exercise also. And enthusiasm for participating in something that is trying to improve things can be found there too.

Is the standard good enough?

Standards may attempt to introduce some rigour into a management process or to specify performance requirements for a product or practice. While it may be demanding to implement the standard as written, the question as to whether the standard is adequate for your needs should be asked. Is the standard setting too low a bar? An industry-led initiative, for example, may be a statement of the practice of the lowest common denominator, rather than something to aspire to.

Conversely, if a product already exceeds the standards specified then there may be little point in any additional work to support meeting a lower standard – unless of course the guarantee that meeting the standard provides (even if it is lower) is necessary to satisfy customers.

Aspirational standards may be written in such a way that their implementation may make no practical difference to the organisation's activities.

But it can be a slog

Implementing a standard, especially throughout a large organisation, can be hard work. There is no denying that part of implementing some standards is a considerable management effort. In particular, the need to demonstrate that every step of a process has been followed can come to seem burdensome. When that happens, the temptation is to work 'on automatic'. That is when the value of the standard, as well as the quality of the paperwork, deteriorates. Rather than some form of sanction for sloppy paperwork, a far better solution is to re-instil the values underlying the purpose of the standard. The goal, after all, is not to fulfil a standard, but to work towards sustainability.

How do you know the standard is making a difference?

Some standards come with a self-assessment built in. Part of the process of conforming to the standard is to review performance against the goals you have set. The ISO management system standards (such as ISO 14001) are of this type. Furthermore, these standards also provide for third parties to assess conformance with them.

But other standards do not set out this kind of process, yet it is still important to assess what difference the standard is making. If you don't know what difference the standard is making, neither will anyone else. It is of very limited value to say to a concerned member of the public, for example, that you follow a standard for sustainability procurement practices if you can't answer the questions as to how much of the procurement falls under the standard or how far the standard has been met in those cases where it has been specified.

As a result, it is important to monitor the implementation of any standard. How that is done will of course vary from one standard to another. The means necessary to monitor the difference that a standard is making should be considered at the start of the implementation process, as it will take far less effort to set up whatever system is necessary at that early stage.

Ask your friends – and enemies

Other people, in other organisations, who have implemented the standard or are doing so, can be a valuable source of advice. In turn of course, you may be asked to give the benefit of your experience to others. The subject of advice may cover anything from the difficulties of managing its implementation to the best way to interpret the more technical aspects of the standard.

In seeking advice, do consider approaching those who are your company's traditional competitors. Because meeting a standard is by definition a consensus activity, the implementation of a standard is not usually a competitive matter. In addition, competitors are likely to understand the context of your questions very well.

Integrate the standard into the business strategy

Most standards will not suffice by themselves as a business strategy! But all standards should feed into that strategy. It is therefore important to be clear how adopting a standard – and working to it – relates to overall business goals. The environmental aspects register within ISO 14001, for example, should relate to the main impacts of the business. It should also be clear, at a high level, how the organisation's business goals will affect achieving the performance governed by the standard.

Sometimes standards are adopted by one organisation because they have been adopted by their competitors. In a weak sense, this does qualify as a 'strategic decision', but it is hardly a sign of great business acumen.

On the other hand, the need for some standards arises fairly directly from strategic business decisions. The growth in standards for labour conditions arose directly out of the decisions to outsource major parts of manufacturing in the 1990s. More recently, further demand for such standards is being felt as a result of the outsourcing of service industry labour.

Do standards, but think stakeholders

While implementing a standard is usually thought of as a management task, it can provide opportunities to reach out to, and benefit from, a wide range of stakeholders. Some standards provide that as part of the very nature of the standard through their governance, particularly those that result from cross-stakeholder co-operation, as does the clothing and footwear standard from the Fair Labor Association (FLA), for example. But even where this is not the case, the standard can be used as a point of departure for discussions with stakeholders.

A richer engagement with stakeholders can bring many benefits. One of the benefits is a higher level of trust between an organisation and its stakeholders. However, a company can also gain useful insights and even business opportunities from stakeholders. Standards can not only provide the opportunity for such interaction, but the process of meeting its constraints and stakeholder demands creatively, may catalyse innovation.

How do standards affect each other?

In considering a new standard, consider how related standards affect each other. The map of standards at the beginning of this book provides a framework for how that could be done. But in any event it is important to work out whether the standard you are considering provides the whole answer to what you are looking for. Or from another angle, how much of another standard, does the one you are considering buy you?

For example, many standards have some kind of reporting requirement. Is it possible to make use of the reporting requirements for the ETI, say, to fulfil the requirements of a GRI report? Or could the aspects register from an ISO 14001 implementation be used to capture and manage a broader set of relevant issues that might derive from ISO 26000?

Make a difference!

Remember to make a difference, rather than put another tick in the standards box. The most important thing is to keep returning to the fact that sustainability standards are intended to make a positive difference to the environment and to people's lives.

For Product Safety Concerns and Information please contact our EU
representative GPSR@taylorandfrancis.com
Taylor & Francis Verlag GmbH, Kaufingerstraße 24, 80331 München, Germany

www.ingramcontent.com/pod-product-compliance
Ingram Content Group UK Ltd.
Pitfield, Milton Keynes, MK11 3LW, UK
UKHW040928180425
457613UK00011B/293